Adam and the
Miraculous

Living Bible Seals

Tony Lasham

MILTON & HUGO L.L.C.
4407 Park Ave., Suite 5
Union City, NJ 07087, USA

Website: *www. miltonandhugo.com*
Hotline: *1- 888-778-0033*
Email: *info@miltonandhugo.com*

Ordering Information:
Quantity sales. Special discounts are granted to corporations, associations, and other organizations. For more information on these discounts, please reach out to the publisher using the contact information provided above.

Library of Congress Control Number: IN-PROCESS
ISBN-13:   979-8-89285-121-3   [Paperback Edition]
                  979-8-89285-122-0   [Digital Edition]

Rev. date: 08/19/2025

Please. Understand that I am not giving up. For years I have been roaming around telling my story to anybody I could get to listen to me, but my efforts have been in vain. I thought I could accomplish this mission if I just put my heart into it and relentlessly push my message upon complete strangers in hopes that God would see my burden and know that I did my best.

This book is a shortcut to reaching as many people as I can in my lifetime and, if that's not enough, the book may someday be recognized as the authentic story of somebody who actually had a past life but died before he could convince the world of its relevance.

CONTENTS

DEDICATION

I'd like to enter the motion that the world nominates a couple to be the King and Queen of the Kingdom of True Love. As King and Queen your only duties will be to go wherever you want and people have to get you whatever you ask for. Of course within reason and with an F.B.I. parallel pursuit so that the rest of the world can keep tabs on them and watch as our wonderful King and Queen mature into immortals and we all can live happily ever after.

The main purpose of this statue is to give Hope to the hard workers around the world who may feel the weight of having a job and the stresses of everyday life. So that they will have a dream to believe in and know that someday anything will be possible.

On that note, Let me be the first to nominate my parents for the job. They are the true spirits of Loyalty and Honesty, key factors in any relationship, and in my personal opinion a match made in Heaven. Leticia and Lloyd Lasham. They did their job by bringing me into this life. Now let them do whatever their hearts desire so we can watch them grow up and we can all mature as a family.

INTRODUCTION

This book is being written for three reasons.

1. As evidence to prove to the F.B.I. that this is a real case of a person having a past life. When I went to them to make my confession I didn't have my game face on and wasn't prepared for the sensitive nature of some of the details. By the time I got to telling the nice lady about what it was like in the Garden of Eden I couldn't hold back the tears. It is hard not to cry when you are confessing the truth and you get the feeling that someone thinks you're crazy. I call that the rapture. So she kindly asked me to leave and have a report made in writing and here it is.

2. So I don't have to repeat myself to every person I meet. I have been to a number of churches in seek of advice on what I should do about my situation only to be told "We don't teach that here, we only know Jesus Christ."

3. To provide a clear set of instructions on what steps have to be taken in order to achieve eternal life… just in case those steps aren't taken in my lifetime… Maybe I should have started the book with that list.

Even I would find it hard to believe if anybody told me they had a past life. But unlike most people I find it offensive because the truth about my having one is quite possibly the most important thing in the world.

I wasn't born with a past life, it came to me through an enigma that holds the proof that with knowledge of the past, comes knowledge of the future.

You see, when I was six years old I cracked The Good Book's Seals and was able to extract so much info from the Bible in less than one day.

Don't worry, I didn't release any plagues upon the Earth or anything. I cracked the Seals in a sense that one would use to crack a joke or a riddle.

I'm hoping that this book will appeal to adventurers, treasure hunters, detectives and just problem solvers in general as I attempt to lay out before you the steps and thought processes that I went through in deciphering the Seals.

I wrote this book with the intention of having the last few chapters to come first, but nobody would have liked it that way so I hope you enjoy the plot twist that comes in the middle of my final piece.

Chapter 1

I cannot take credit for every line in this composition. Although I am the first known source on Earth. Most of my writing comes from divine origin.

For example:

There is no such thing as trouble...

Picture yourself standing on the edge of a rocky seashore where you can see a lighthouse on a cliff ahead of you and the turbulent waters of the ocean churning far below you. On the horizon a storm is brewing.

Doesn't that make you want to set a course and reach your destination? Trouble doubles inspiration.

On the other hand, feats of great strength and impossible stunts like leaping a building in a single bound, stopping a speeding bullet train or walking on water seizes our hearts and puts a freeze over our souls as we know we would never be able to accomplish such a task in real life. Sometimes inspiration can double the trouble.

While I'm on the subject of sea shores did you know that footprints of Adam's story can be found to this day in the shimmering sands of the beach in the form of common sense sand dollars that were cast in the two halves of the mold that God broke after He created Adam.

All of mankind after that was created with the same skeletal sound frame of mind able to tell the differences between good and wrong in the *decency* life forms but they are sensitive to their surroundings and don't like to make waves.

This is only half of the enigma,
you see, with knowledge of the past comes
knowledge of the future.

The first chapter of this book is dedicated to the world, the way God dreamed it would be, and the sciences that would have taken mankind thousands upon thousands of years to stumble across in nature. I was going to make this chapter last but since it IS the most important I rearranged my book to make it the first chapter.

1. Work every other day shifts. You wake up every day in a different world.

You want to work every other day because of this... When you go to work you are giving your light to the world, but what is one flame in a sea of lights, just a candle blowing in the wind.

But, on your days off you can focus that light on your immediate family and relatively close acquaintances and it becomes like a heat lamp on your whole world. That is why, even though we haven't switched to this system yet, you should still try to pretend you are already working those every other day shifts because by believing that is how it is you can reap the benefits in knowing that is how it always was and always will be.

Not to mention everybody still gets 2 days off in a row on the weekends Sabbath. Your two days would either be Saturday and Sunday or Sunday and Monday because everybody is off on Sundays. Bonus world to wake up in? Heaven possibly? If we don't try, how will we ever find out?

2. I was shown how we could raise our children through a program called the two-way mirror program. That is a program where children are taken from their parents at a young age and raised on islands called nursery isles where they sit with and learn how to behave from fully grown midgets. Never underestimate the power of the little people. Well they mostly run around and play until they are ready to start work and go to school and because every child develops at his or her own speed there is no pressure for them to start school right away.

The parents can still be a part of their children's lives as a teacher, a mailman or bagger at the local grocery store or something. The difference between that life and this one is that one day you wake up and realize you are never alone and the world surrounding you is your family and if the parents decide to keep it a secret the child will never have to experience the loss of a loved one. At the right age, maybe 7, the kids would be given simple chores like watering the horses or feeding the chickens. The point is to instill a sense of responsibility in them and for them to know that someday they will have an important job that someone's life depends on them doing.

The best thing about it is that when they graduate into the workforce, it is a foreign on the job training exchange program, where you go through life from job to job, changing to a new one whenever it seems prudent, until you find something you have a knack for and hopefully turn that love for the job into your nick.

So Nursery Isle then Nick and Knack.

3. There should be a ceremony that happens once every ten years where all of the churches get together to marry couples, maybe you could get married five times, once at each church.

The ceremony should include a handing out of medals and we should make up ten new laws every ten years that the whole world can live by. Easy enough?

4. And another thing we should recognize is how the church should be separated into two sects. And I will tell two secrets to the women that they will keep from the men and the men will have secrets to keep from the women. The power of these secrets will be woven into the fabric of our life.

5. Another thing to put on the agenda is about a crime that was committed against an entire race that the whole world hasn't made up for and I know how we can fix the grudges and spite left from those scars.

There was a horrific crime that was committed against an entire race and all we did to correct it was stop doing it, in other words we did nothing to right the wrong and redeem ourselves.

This is our chance to pay it forward. God is so powerful that on top of everything that we have the rite to fix in the world he created a way for us to redeem ourselves from something we haven't even done. Here's my proposition.

We look at every country in the global neighborhood as if it has the right to let its land be inhabited by people from any other foreign country. And in order to make things right there should be one country that has the right to deny letting anybody from another country inhabit it without Royal Invitation.

This would be a way to achieve our redemption while at the same time making every other country in the world feel more royal as individual members of a global community.

6. I also want to be sure to mention the "Grambars" of justice before I finish this book. You see, for every sentence passed in court there is a "grambar" that goes on one of two sides of the blind scales of justice, one side is labeled as rewards and the other side is labeled consequences. There should be more rewards awarded in court and that is why it may seem at times like corruption is winning. A lot to think about.

7. Don't forget the one that I mentioned in the Dedication to this book!

8. Destroy Peace. When we examine the second word in the first Seal, we can conclude that judgment is either fact or opinion. Like a seed that sprouts up into two branches, either faith or belief. Faith is putting all of your eggs in one basket and looking up to a higher power with no understanding, while believing is knowing that you are the one who God is counting on. Sound familiar? In God We Trust!

The word Faith is called a flair spell because when you first see it, it lights up the sky and inspires us to dream to new heights. But as the flair descends and is consumed by the impenetrable darkness, you realize that someone is in distress.

There are 2 other flair spells I know of. One is the word "Universe," because it holds the promise of vast wealth at the same time personifying the personification of solitary solitude. I think it is much wiser to get rid of that word completely from your vocabulary and replace it with "Galaxy."

And the other word is "Peace." Because if it wasn't a word there wouldn't be a meaning for the opposite, War. I say replace it with the word "Harmony" and watch how much more intellectual our galaxy becomes!

9. Kids should be split up into pairs and told that their partner is the only other person you can count on for everything for the rest of your life (after leaving the nursery aisle of course). You two are the only things you've got to count on in this world. It would be a good exercise in learning what it feels like to have to depend on somebody else. It would also teach them each how to be trustworthy and what happens when you let somebody down. They would learn how to break up using what is called the "Washaking Hands" method where sometimes you have to be sensitive towards others emotions to avoid any hard feelings between each other down the road.

10. Last but not least tap the mountain secretes before they are locked away forever.

And put our family pods in ranks of order that start with the Mother and Father on top and go from first born boy to youngest boy on the male side but ascends from youngest daughter to oldest daughter on the female side.

Chapter 2

Total Recall

After cracking the seals, for three nights in a row I woke up to the feeling that I had a dream but I was unable to remember anything about it.

The only thing I was certain about is that I spent the whole night long staring up at a starless sky.

I thought nothing of it and went on with my morning routine of getting ready for school.

On the third day the same thing happened and I caught the bus to school.

On the way home after school I caught the wrong bus and my parents had to come pick me up at the school district. It was during the ride home in our family station wagon that the memories of a life before this one came rushing back. At first I saw myself as a baby, observing what a day was and becoming familiar with the fact that there was a day yesterday and that there would be another one tomorrow.

I remember whenever I'd wake up as a baby, the reason that I would cry so much... I was coming from a place in Heaven where all my friends were and I knew I would be forgetting them permanently.

I remembered being in my mother's womb and seeing the voices of her and my father dominating the horizon as visual sound waves that went all the way across my peripheral vision.

And then it got scary.

I saw a horrible scene, too horrible to testify, where thousands died at the end of the world when it was destroyed by water. Then the vision went back to when we were wandering aimlessly through the desert. And then it went even further back to a community that lived at the base of a pyramid.

Earlier than that the vision took me through an underground territory, through the halls of knowledge and all the way back to a place called Eden. And even further more than that.

The flashback went all the way back to the beginning of time and to my surprise, when it got to the very beginning I just remembered the whole thing like I actually lived through it. Even the emotions that the main character was feeling whenever he had to make a decision, I remembered it all like it was yesterday!

I tried to get my mother's attention and almost told her the miracle that I just witnessed right then and there but it was like a precious gem of my soul and I thought I might be risking my life if I told either of my parents anything.

"If it was true then there would have to be other people who shared the same experience living and walking on Earth right now" I reasoned with myself.

So I decided to keep it to myself until I could find these other people whom I shared the secret with.

That was possibly the most selfish thing I ever did and I think it came with its own consequences. Now, no matter how hard I try to convince them my story is true, they don't believe me.

For some mysterious reason the memory of my past life went away and I never had a second thought about it. Until a couple of years later.

We were a military family so this part of the story happened in a totally new neighborhood in the United States…

…I had another chance to reveal my secret in the middle of a friendly neighborhood game of catch. I was with my friends when the memory came flooding back and I dropped everything to run home to let my mom in on it.

I raced down the street not bothering to look both ways before crossing but as I reached the threshold of our home this thought occurred to me, "I was just having fun with my friends and now my life is going to be full of responsibility" and I once again made up an excuse for not telling anybody. Reasoning "If it is my destiny to change the world then it will happen sooner or later, no matter what." And as quickly as it returned the memory of the vision went away, like an uninvited visitor.

As it would happen I had a wonderful childhood and teenage years. By the third time the memory came back, I was so aware of what other people thought of each other that I couldn't confess my secret without thinking somebody would call me crazy.

So, to review, it was not a dream because I was wide awake when the experience returned to me. I discovered the Seals before I received this flashback. And here is my story and this is where the movie should start from. I'll tell you about the Seals afterwards.

Chapter 3

The Story Begins

The next few chapters happens in a world before word existed.

At first there wasn't anything around for a long, long time. No stars, no planets, no nothing. All there was, was this vast void and silence. Not even God knew He existed yet.

It remained this way for eons.

A seemingly endless amount of eternities passed before Time made a complete revolution through Infinity back to the point in existence where it started its journey of eternities just to start a new one over again.

There is no way of knowing how many times this eternal cycle of infinite eternities had gone by unnoticed before God became conscious that even Time existed and He stirred from His eternal slumber and saw that the world was flat like a clean slate and that all was well and it was good.

There wasn't much of anything around the world and it might have been more than a few revolutions through eternity before our Creator had a mind to change anything.

The world was calm and flat, like a dark theater before the movie begins.

The only motion that could be detected was around the edges of the world, it was like the world was on a parade floating through the corridors of time.

So nothing changed for a very long time. An eternity passed and another began. There are eternal eternities in one infinity and still nothing changed. Until one day God said "This place is plank boredom. We need something to lighten up the place."

And with that bright idea there was light. It was like a dazzling jewel that pierced the fabric of the night's sky.

You could view it from as far or as close up as you'd want to. And named for star general Decoration, Ray for short, but unfortunately the novelty of it eventually wore off.

Bored again (after a few eternities) with the light, before you could think the light shot off making a line that started from the center of the world and continued forever outwardly in a straight line, never reaching the edge.

No matter how long the line got there was always enough distance for God to back up and the line would seem as if it were starting its journey over again.

Eventually the fun of this also wore off and the next rational thing that would happen did. The ray, that was once only a point in the middle of the world, shot off in the opposite direction.

Now this changes everything because eventually one or most likely both of the traveling lines will reach the edge. No matter how far you back up in the distance this time there is no way to avoid it.

What happened when each of the lines struck into either edge is they vanished for a split second and reappeared at a random point on the map and continued on its course.

At first there wasn't much difference to the makeup of the world since the very beginning, but that would soon change. The light was taking up more and more space and there was nothing to stop it.

The lines criss-crossed back and forth over the dark firmament so much that there were barely any spaces left that weren't light. Until finally there was only one spot that was left to be hit by light. There is no exact way of saying how many times the light would cut across the world back and forth before the last spot of darkness was struck, there may have been many times that we were sure that the light was coming towards that one last spot but just barely missed it.

It seemed like another eternity before it came by again and it still missed.

Until that last time when it finally did hit it and the world exploded into three dimensions. Static electricity and life spread like wildfire. As the dust settled, lower life forms picked ground rules to lord over and became Higher Powers, claiming the titles of Gods. One of the Gods, The Lord of Morality who has power over immortality, boasts such power to hold back life from existing and He did.

That was when the Gods took their time and designed Creation. The next chapter describes an era that the God's had the power to make exist before the beginning of Time and before the story of light.

Chapter 4

Introduction To The Gods

In all of The God's vast wells of knowledge and reflection pools of wisdom They reasoned that if there was going to be a Creation there would have to be a Destruction so They went back to an era that existed before the story of light and made Destruction come first.

From a point of view above the Earth where I could see the curvature of it in the far off distance, I saw below me the figure of a person standing in a field.

Before him were crops planted in neat rows and behind him was the edge of the wilderness. Beyond the crop patterns there was a sidewalk that led past a fenced in out-door court to a schoolhouse complete with a bell tower.

The peaceful scene was disturbed when an earth shaking boom shook the world, knocking the figure who stood in the open meadow to his knees.

Looking up to the sky to see the source of the commotion I witnessed the imprint of one ring miles in diameter planted in the sky.

Shortly after another earth shaking boom announced another ring that intersected the first one.

While pieces of the sky were still falling to the ground, the last of three devastating blows hit leaving something like the Olympic rings symbol stamped across the sky.

The next thing I heard was someone trying to start an internal combustion engine. After a couple of unsuccessful tries the motor roared into life.

Sharp teeth spinning on a blade appeared from behind the sky and continued to cut diagonally downward from right to left across the three rings.

Yet again the powerful internal combustion engine revved and the sword made another pass over the O's completing an enormous X hundreds of miles across the sky.

It was calm again for a few seconds before the sound of footsteps started pounding from some unknown location below the rafters of Heaven. At a slow pace they faded away into the distance and just before they were so faint that you could barely hear them they began to make a turn.

The urgency in them as they grew louder and louder. Each step building up speed as they got closer and closer becoming so intense that you couldn't hear yourself think.

With a tremendous crash the head of a ram on a human-like giant body exploded through the sky.

This was the God of Strength.

After removing His head from the hole, the horse-headed Lord of Morality was visible in the drywall of the sky.

He clicked His tongue and tipped His hat and that was all the introduction that the God's needed before they began doing Their work.

The black smith aprons they wore and knee length short pants did little to hide their muscular physiques.

With a swing of His war mallet one of the pillars of Heaven disintegrated into little pieces like a volcano.

On either side of the universe two dragons soared through the heavens eating their way through whatever existed until there was nothing left.

They are the 2 Neutral Gods of War, Puff and Duplitricon. One of them had a body made of clouds while the other looked like a conveyor belt that zig-zagged back and forth across the cosmos.

(They are always in competition with each other, trying to see who can get the most points. Like the best of enemies.)

The Goddess Destiny took the form of a great white dove casting Her Rays of Destruction down from high above for the world to for the lone figure to bask in.

As far as you could see and more, from corner to corner The Lord of Morality and His Army of Force men God's dismantled every inch of what existed. Even the curvature of the Earth was nothing more than a memory.

A good humor giraffe-headed God complete with astronaut helmet was there with a push broom sweeping all of the debris into a throne where Father Time would later sit before the figure who stood in the meadow to witness the great event.

On the footrest before God's throne, the lone figure who once stood in the meadow now laid in the fetal position holding his head in his hands weeping. Pants and shirt sleeves ripped to tattered ribbons from all of the demolition, the figure basked in awe from the majestic power of God's glory.

The Gods made me memorize one word that contained all of their names.

Harmburgerrawkgardennyltickapheobebellzeebeebop

Don't quote me on that being exactly right. We practiced so many times and I always had to start over so by the 50ᵗʰ time They're all just going "Say hamburger, rock garden…" so that it would be easier to remember.

Chapter 5

Back to the Beginning

There were so many versions of reality. One where the red team fed on the green team. So the green team had to have some super defenses like a triceratops to take the lead in the herd, brontosauruses on the sides of the pack to protect their young in the center of the clutch and even a stegosaurus with its hammer tail to protect the rear.

Who knows what Good and Evil will come up with next. All I know is that the first creation wasn't as well planned out as this one is now.

There were no walls, ceilings or floors. Winged beasts of every kind chased each other around and in the center of the universe hovered God like an island.

On the shoulders of this massive island there were the graven images of our Creators.

Once life was let loose on creation again (after it was stopped at the end of Chapter 5) the Creator's creatures scattered to the furthest corners of the galaxy, never to be seen again in the presence of God, who cared so much about them.

A remorseful God destroyed that version of creation with fire in almost the same instant that He created it.

But Eden was different. A lot of thought was put into this version of Creation.

Every creature was firmly grounded in the detention of earth. Each plant had their own individual geometric design and the sky! The sky was painted the pink and baby blue hues of eternal twilight.

The first creature allowed to roam freely through the Garden of Eden was a unicorn named Leonardo. You should remember this name because it stands for something. The First Sun King. His one horn also was representative of the number 1.

Although allowed to roam wherever He wanted to, Leonardo never really did much of anything. The only thing that he did was sit in one spot all day just staring at the fallen leaves on the ground. You might think that Leo was a statue or something because he remained in that position for ages. Honestly, just sit there and gaze at dead leaves forever and ever in awe of Existence.

God took matters into His own hands and after deciding the best option was for Leo to have a playmate. So He put Leo in a deep sleep and brought him to the dark side of the moon, which is the furthest place in the universe from Earth, and split him right down the middle. And that is where Leo's better half, Joy came from.

But it was to no avail. Nothing changed. Life returned to the same old routine of Leo stuck in his never ending ground gazing.

Once, Joy even did a running jump and rolled right in front of him trying to get him to frolic with her but all he did was smile, acknowledged her and went back to staring at the ground.

Then came along the Serpent to help. Maybe she was God's idea. In the Book of Names a picture of the serpent's mouth can be seen cracking open exposing her teeth and a puff of smoke exhaled from the mouth dissipates into the air spelling out her name, Glamourahhh.

If you're thinking that the serpent was some sort of garden variety legless viper then I'm afraid you couldn't be more mistaken.

The sublime beauty of the serpent surpasses that of any unicorn by far.

Glamourah walked upright with two different hind legs, one reptilian and the other bird-like. She had a black armor plated body and a very snake-like head. In her wiry kinky tail she held orbs and galaxies that resembled solar systems and subatomic particles. But the most unforgettable feature of the serpent was the long thin whips that were its forelegs.

Before she entered any scene, a clock like "Clippity cloppitty" would announce her arrival.

Once she did a trick for us, tapping the ground with a single one of her fore ribbons creating a ring of dust to spring from the spot she tapped that spread like a mushroom cloud after an atomic bomb exploded, only on a miniature scale.

But still all Leo ever did was bask in awe of being alive.

One day Leo noticed that his playmates weren't around and he went off to find them. After some time he began to panic and frantically began racing to and fro looking high and low everywhere to find them. That was when he heard a little bird up in a tree ask what was the matter.

It was written all over his face, he was so worried about where his playmates were.

"Oh them," Robin chirped, "they're at the Old Well around the bend." Not wasting a minute to say thanks, Leo rushed off to see what was going on.

A steady flow of water trickled down a sheer ridge full of live foliage and gathered into a circle of rocks at the base of the cliff known as The Old Well.

When he got there he found the serpent trying to coax Joy into taking a sip from the fountain.

Leo thought it was a trick and argued with her hoping she would see it was a bad idea but the serpent was persistent and she found herself more and more confused. The more they fought the less she seemed to know what to do. I guess when the choice comes down to "do something" or "do nothing" it's easier to do something than nothing so she bowed her head down to take a sip.

That was when the picturesque scene began to dance with electricity. The water began to steam into a vapor releasing sparks into the air and vibrant light made the atmosphere glow a little brighter than before.

Joy's body was covered in a sheer energy causing her spirit to dissolve into the air where she was transported from where she was standing to a new spot hovering above the center of the fountain.

No longer a unicorn, her body was cloaked in a dark hooded robe and she now had the face of a woman. It was the most enchanting creature Leonardo had ever seen. The last thing he saw of her was a look of despair as she brought both of her hands up to her face and vanished down the fountain.

Leo, stricken with sadness, thought there was no point in going on. Giving up on life without his soul mate he lowered his head to take a lap.

The same thing that happened to Joy happened to him only this time when he hovered above the well he witnessed a powerful blizzard sweep in and the last glimpse he caught of Eden was all of its trees being coated in snow.

And when the Garden of Eden's title became the Kingdom of Heaven, so did Leonardo's name also change into Able.

Chapter 6

Below Eden

The next thing you know Able found himself in the Halls of Knowledge which is a corridor that goes on and on with no twists or turns for ever and ever. Sort of like the entrance to The Labyrinth.

A shadowy figure of a maiden crossed Able's path, emerging from a wall on the left then dissolving into the wall on the right. To Able's amazement the woman's hand reemerged from the wall on the right and Able grabbed a hold of it drawing him through the same wall.

On the other side of the wall, Able found himself once again alone in a strange underground cavern.

He heard voices talking in the distance and opted to investigate.

When he got to the source of the chatter he found himself in the company of druids who were all dressed in the same sack cloth as he was ever since the transformation due to The Old Well.

One particular druid, I'll just call him Darius, was giving out orders for all of his congregation to follow and they slowly made their way out of this territory into the land of Mesopotamia.

Along one tunnel there was a tapestry depicting what was going on as the entourage made its way to the cavern entrance. Like a live view of current events tapestry.

Now known to go by the name of Able, all he had to do to regain entry into the Kingdom of Heaven was spread the Glory of God's Kingdom.

Life was so surreal and tranquil. The days were spent sculpting sandstone busts with their bare hands. All you needed was a chisel to be held in your free hand and you could carve the cheek of a statue with your bare hand.

But Able thought it was wrong for the Pharaoh to enslave the people of this civilization in such a way that they had to do tasks and carve sculptures against their will.

With a crook in his finger between his lips, he ushered the people away from the safety of Mesopotamia, into the desert where they would seek out a better life.

This was the sin that earned Able a new name. Because he committed another sin by endangering the lives of his people the conditions for his return back into Heaven changed. Not only did he have to spread the Glory of God's Kingdom but now he would have to accomplish that task in secrecy. And he was now known by the name of Moses.

...Wandering through the desert Moses got the idea to ask God for guidance and he climbed into a bush to ask God for his help. But language wasn't as advanced then as it is today and they had a hard time communicating their thoughts. Back then the only form of communication was called "Expressionment" where if you had a question you would look someone in the face and try your best to use empathy for the desired result.

The conversation between God and Moses went like this. Moses would look up to the sky with a desperate look on his face and implore God for assistance. To which God did the only thing He could do back then and that was write squiggly lines in the sky hoping Moses would understand.

Satisfied that he thought he knew what God was saying Moses returned to his people and told them "We should all split up, go in different directions so that the Pharaoh couldn't track them and meet up back at the pyramid to await the coming of God."

When the plan worked and they all met up again at the pyramid God was angry because they left the Pharaoh out of the celebration causing the Pharaoh to shed a tear.

Well in God's eyes one tear is as good as bloodshed and the world was destroyed because of that.

A mountain far off in the distance seemed to rise from the ground and began to close in on the scene at the end of the world. Slowly, one by one iridescent eyes appeared on the mountain peaks, glowing a ghostly orange tinge.

The mountain stretched across the horizon and rose to unbelievable heights when two forks of lightning struck sideways from east to west below the summits and peaks.

The lines left behind by the lightning became mouths and one began to speak, "I am the Alpha and the Omega, the first last and always will be…" Then bodies started falling from the sky and were swallowed up by the second mouth while the first kept talking.

They took turns talking and eating and deep inside of the mouths you could see two lakes of fire where people were being burned alive. Moses took it so hard, he was the one that led the world to its end, he was the one responsible for this terrible fate. The guilt was too much for him and he fell on his face and began wailing and crying like a baby.

So strong was his downpour of tears that the ground became soaked with tears.

Nothing could stop his weeping and the puddles became pools and the world started to get flooded. He cried so much that the world became filled with water and the Holy Ghost showed up and took mercy upon his soul, creating an ark to be the vessel of his spirit and finally dubbing the poor man Noah.

This is the truth and what I believe to be the mystery of name. You'll notice I never said his name was Adam. The first time I heard of the name Adam was in this lifetime. Isn't it funny how one little lie can make you hunger for the whole truth and nothing but the truth.

If you believe me please take my first chapter into consideration when making plans for the future of this planet.

Chapter 7

The Invisible Scrolls

May the divine order of the scrolls teach our children to be volunteers that will mature into helpers and one day have the power to grant anyone their wishes if only for ten seconds before they graduate into Paladins.

Three days before chapter two (In this lifetime)...

...Ten feet from the Bible I stood in awe of how something could be so powerful that it causes people all over the world to put on their best Sunday outfits and flock to temples of worship once a week.

I wondered if it was a manmade book or some kind of supernatural phenomenon that was the source of this mystical tome's origin. These are the series of questions that I asked myself in seeking out the truth that actually ended up in me summoning a Higher Power.

First, I wondered "What would the world be like if the Bible didn't exist?" and as if to answer my query a vision of a world at war where savages fought over borders with sticks and stones was conjured in my head. I saw the world consumed in the flames of Chaos.

Next I asked myself "Where in the universe would God be if the Bible didn't exist?" because it is His life line and without it nobody would believe in Him or even know He existed.

And that was when I felt the presence of another being enter the room I was previously alone with the Bible in.

It was no mere hunch or suspicious feeling that something else had entered the room. It was a full blown "Oh kaka… Now I'm in trouble!" impending doom vibe.

The entity knew I knew it was there but that wasn't enough. It projected an aura of complete dominance over me and I crumpled beneath Its weight.

For several seconds It imposed Its omnipotent presence down upon me from the vantage point that It must have hovered from. I was powerless against the psychic attack and my body bent to Its will into a crouching position. One knee on the ground and one hand over my right pants pocket, I got the feeling that this was exactly how It wanted me to remain. Out of control of my own limbs. My mind raced with thoughts of how I was ever going to get out of this alive and tears were about to flow in my watering eyes.

But just when things seemed to be at their worst I had an epiphany. "How can I give my life in service to You in order to prove I was worth receiving the gift (of life) in the first place?" I thought and tears of self-preservation turned to tears of joy with the anticipation of working for the most awesome boss in the universe.

That must've done the trick because as my anguish and remorse turned to a more bashful and slightly embarrassed feeling.

Then I got the sense that the Being wanted to say something.

The prospect that this entity actually wanted to communicate with a lower life form like me was too much to comprehend.

Overjoyed, I opened every pore in my body so that I might absorb whatever great wisdom this God was about to bestow upon me.

I wondered how an all knowing super being was going to start a conversation with me.

I tried to the best of my ability to understand that there would have to be an alphabet with symbols for sounds that we would have to put together to form words and then complete sentences.

As my mind raced to figure all these variables I almost missed His message.

"Don't judge a blah blah blah blah."

But in my best attempt to not miss a single morsel of meaning I ended up getting stuck on the very first word and the rest of the sentence meant nothing to me.

It was more like "Don't! Judge a book by it's cover." Because how could any sentence that begins with the meaning for the word "Don't" be more than one word long. You have to think about the meaning before you move on and I got stuck.

From here it gets very difficult to explain because I entered a trancelike state and deciphered a whole lot of understanding for the word. Like a great well bursting at the seams with water I drank from the spell called "Don't" and did so until my thirst for curiosity was quenched.

I saw these words appear before me in thin air:

"Nursery rhymes, fairy tales, myths and fables all come from a place older than man's first set of footprints on Earth."

So much information was deciphered in that trance that it is hard to tell exactly which bit of it came first while I was in it.

Do you want to know one of the more clever things I found in this spell? The Missing Archery Bunker, not missing *link* mind you. Bunker.

You just ask yourself what character stands out the most in this line up of letters and then follow through with the same question. Good detective strategy.

So, I figured why do all of these letters have fancy make up to symbolize a simple sound while the apostrophe is just a little dash with a big name?

The next thing I did was ask myself "What syllable stood out the most in the word apostrophe?" and my instincts told me it was the "post" that was the most prominent.

That was when I got a cue from God... He asked me *"What is the opposite of the top spot of a post?"*

After some time in deep thought I visualized an old post fort being constructed and saw that the bottom of the posts that were in a wagon and all of the posts had been sharpened to a point on the bottom.

So I imagined the holes being dug in the shape of a "V" and came to the conclusion that the opposite of the top spot of a post was a divot. And because golfing ranges have divots in them from the golfer swinging the driver off the tee, it seemed to make sense. I found The Missing Archery Bunker!

This is how close my relationship with God is. You may doubt that God has the reach or would even bother going so far as to plant this hidden jewel in his works but I see it as a sign of a foundation to a bridge between Heaven and Earth that holds the promise that the long goner that left it here still remains.

If you ever make it out of the trap spell "Don't" you will find another lesson in all of the words that have a meaning for the sound "By."

As you contemplate all of their possible meanings, try to hold each one in your head at once and with a little hard work a vision will appear in your mind of a long row of capital letter "I's."

Don't be afraid. It's just a lecture about how we all are individual charges with responsibilities and how we can be in someone else's charge or have charges under us. I guess the point of that lecture is that divine power comes from Heaven and we are all in Heaven's charge.

I hope you will enjoy it, I hate to give away a free lesson! After I spent a sufficient amount of time in the trance researching the word "Don't" I ventured forth wearily, inch by inch, letter by letter.

I would go "Don't J." and think about all of the aspects that a single letter had on the impact of the whole sentence. Then I would go "Don't J-U." and always race back to the safety of the spell "Don't" alone, because I hadn't been struck dead by a bolt of lightning yet. It was like being safe or on base.

Eventually I got to "Don't judge job..." and my patience was overpowered by my curiosity and I just had to sprint to the end of the sentence justifying my actions by telling myself it was worth suffering the penalty of death if it meant getting to know my God better.

That was when I saw the most amazing thing. An invisible scroll. As if God knew I would be past my mental breaking point at the exact part of the sentence when I decided to sprint to the end of the cliché, all of the syllables, symbols and synonyms got bunched together and it read out before my eyes:

"Don't judge a bad job nosy busy bodies even want."

My Bible trade route.

I had a second to second guess my own eyes, but how could I deny the fact that I had just read a sentence that wasn't there a moment ago. I had to believe in God with all my might, because there was no way that I could put my faith in the wrong place by saying the Devil made me see it.

Finally free from the Trap Spell "Don't" I felt like it was God's way of rewarding me with a gift for being so disciplined. I call it the gift of "infra red herring vision" because it has led me to so many clues that were pertinent in solving this whole mystery.

In my astonishment from actually seeing an invisible scroll, my curiosity piqued and I became obsessed with them, knowing that there must be more out there. And I found several. One goes:

"What does the first rule a good book covers offer for you to afford your ability to purchase and maintain traction while scaling glossy areas?"

But the first one I found immediately after the badge job one goes:

"Don't continue main attempt... (seeing those words alone definitely gave me the sense of some hidden meaning)...in putting an outlet on a chore you were originally aware about... (notch your arrow)... where the quick river rapids are the same as the deep current flow."

Finally, we are still ten feet from the Bible and we get to the word "cover."

This is as close to the Bible that you can get before realizing that you are lost because the trail just ends there.

Like a detective that followed a lead while solving a case, this word seems to be a dead end or a red herring. But if we meditate on the word "cover" and try thinking about it, the only thing that God knew would be here at this dead end was "You" and the word "cover," the next step in solving the case reveals itself.

Wait. I take that back. One other important clue has bearing on solving this mystery and that clue is the word "cliche."

I should have mentioned this earlier. The first time I ever heard the phrase "Don't judge a book by it's cover" I was alone, (with a higher power) and I instinctively knew it was a cliche. But what amazed me even more was the fact that the word cliche was in my vocabulary! To my surprise there were also some cliches I had never heard before floating around in my vocabulary but I thought that it was just something everybody has sewn into their genes.

Back to the last word in the first seal, cover. You've followed all the clues to this dead end but where do you go from here?

The only things we know God would know would be here when you got this far is you and the word cover. There is know way of God predicting what you would be wearing, if anything at all so why look so hard for a hint if this is really the path that God left for us to find?

What are you covered in? Skin, right? So the next clue is the cliché "Beauty is only skin deep." But the most important word in the second seal is the second word "is."

Try to think of any other cliches where the second word can be deciphered into a question and I think you will be surprised at what you will find.

These are the three invisible scrolls that I found in "You are what you eat," "Looks can be deceiving," and "Beauty is only skin deep." The second word in each one of these cliches is what emphasizes the word "Second" in the second seal.

"You are what you eat, no waiter. I'm planning on boiled eggs salted for breakfast."

"Look scan be a bead (BB) in a bean neck claspet."

And... (saved the best for last)

"A true beaut is a kin's encrusted sword dipped in a dragon's smile, as old as the knight's code of dependency."

And everybody knows what happens if you submerge a rusty sword in green slime, right? Then I don't have to explain it to you.

There are multiple scrolls you can find for each of these cliches just go through them word by word and stop to think about anything that makes you think. One that I am particularly impressed with goes:

"Beauty is a needle's eye sewn from between me and to you too."

Even more impressive this one is:

"Beauty is a radius radiated from a pin point above a hole in a record album label."

And the fourth spell level, finally racing from the cover to page one is, "Read between the lines."

I consider this one to be priceless as to the wealth of information that can be deciphered in this "given." An alternative dungeon guide's way of saying you're on the right track because alter"native" guides might make you think of Indians and Indian "giving."

There are many signs pointing to God's benevolence for native guides. You might think of cliches as echoes and as a way to communicate over long distances, in other words an ancient Indian tracker Relic location devise.

There are several hidden puzzles that you can find the solution to in the phrase "Read between the lines." I found four of them. Here's one for free.

If you were to think outside of the box, and rearrange the words "Read between the lines, you might come up with this solution. Draw a line between the word "Read."

Now ask yourself "If Re and Ad represented Good and Evil, which one would be which and why? It's sort of like the puzzle in "Don't" where you find yourself unable to advance or retreat so you do the next sensible thing and flip over the middle letter. Do you know what I mean? Think about for a while and you might find that the word "Dou" foreshadows an ancient battle between your mind and your heart.

So, you go halfway across the drawbridge in "Don't" then fall in the moat where you use the second seal like a staircase and finally find yourself on the first page you "Read" (because "Read between the lines" is another pocket puzzle) and eventually you will find yourself at the first letter of the Bible, the capital letter I "In the beginning" this is w\the invisible scroll that I saw after some time in thought about the capital letter "I.":

"In the beckoning candle's lit area pylon up under rubble of foundation as a token to pay of meant gratitude to the amplifier of my life."

Do you see why "Don't judge a bad job nosey busy bodies even wants" is so important? Because you shouldn't pass sentence anyway and it dents your sharp focus just enough for you to understand and accept the wisdom that these invisible scrolls have to offer.

To me what stands out is the "pylon of honorable foundation" in the middle and "the apple of my eye" at the end, not to mention the candle slit where a token might go.

Another one I found in this letter goes:

"What meaning estimatedely directly defines the capital letter I's to "in."

There are a couple more in there for you to find on your own. Like…

How much comprehension did the composer compress into the composition of the word "The?"

Another cue I got from God at about the same time I made it to the first letter of Genesis came in the form of this question: "What waterfowl left its tracks behind in the first letter of the Bible?" I'll reveal the answer later.

It's hard to say but God will never make it so hard that you can't figure it out. There is a hint in the question.

So that's the first letter. Now onto the second one, the lowercase letter c!

Chapter 8

When a Peg Falls Entry

The second letter in the Bible you might think is easy to find but it requires quite a great deal of thought and creativity to find. Surely you would think that if the first letter in the book is "I" the second letter must be on the last page because beauty is only skin deep so, following that logic we skip to the last page only to discover the last word in the Bible is "Amen."

How could that be? I'm hunting down this great all-knowing being and He makes the last letter in His Book the same exact letter as the second letter in the word "In?"

It's too great of a coincidence if you ask me.

I must be acting too sharply or using too much guiltiness. As if there is an answer to my calling but I am too demanding, exacting my wish and forcing God to give me the answer I am looking for without even being worthy of it.

I decided to take my own cue and let one of my eyes get out of focus so I could perform a more thorough investigation of the crime scene or excavation dig site if you will.

The first thing you notice when you do that (let one of your eyes cross) is that the ink on the page that made up the words become blotted like tiny storm clouds and it is the space between the words that stands out the most.

I began seeing the effect of rain drops on a window or a windshield that would bump into each other at the top of the page, gain mass and then streak all the way to the bottom of the page.

I assumed I was being too strict with my research and ended up flipping a page or two in the last chapter.

The once stable rain drops that streaked to the bottom of the pages picked up speed giving the effect of lightning strikes complete with forks and I turned another two or three pages.

After a couple more lightning strikes and three more pages something strange happened when the bolts of lightning crossed each other forming a giant "X" that took up two pages. I let my lazy eye come back into focus and concentrated my gaze onto the point where the two forks crossed to find the beginning of this quote in Revelations: "Come up hither…"

I pride myself in knowing why this letter should be considered a lower case letter and explaining would only waste valuable time of which I have a limited supply of. Just take my word for it and try to hold that letter with God's Reach.

This was when I got another cue from God in the form of a strange riddle that goes "How does the consonant letter "c" appear in the middle lane elementary grammar pizza purple?" (piece of paper) Try to find for yourself before you read beyond this. Here. Stop, look and listen.

If you imagine the lowercase letter c written in the middle of an elementary ruled grammar paper you might notice that it appears to be looking up to the letter, whatever letter would be next to it. Co-inspirational if I do say so myself. And that's how I found out that dungeon phases are coined in phrases.

How's the graphics on this scroll I found in my floating junk?:

"How big does the mysterious stump of life have to be to support a flip co-intentional land turn table on it?" If you use your mind's eye to look closer for the answer to this riddle you might see God's way of saying "Hi."

Would you believe the third letter is "A?"

"And now the Serpent was subtle and cunning."

When you reach this entry in Genesis, It becomes apparent that we should take heed if you believe in the power of God it's just a good idea.

The two invisible scrolls I obtained from this letter have nothing to do with the word "And."

The first one goes…

"By men under looking hard for adoring good is a track meant to wise under God."

And…

"Up honest trails lined in sin you see where th whore nets it's sting." or something like that.

That's it. The three letters that I found invisible scrolls in. The capital letter I, the lowercase c and the A in "And now the serpent was subtle and cunning.

So, those are the letters from the Bible I found invisible scrolls in. The "I" the "c" and the "A." Fascinating enough?

The Icy Hand of God "In" "Come" "And!"

Chapter 9

The Hallway Bookcase Shelf Fall Slide Into Second Basic Commandment.

When I tried rearranging the seven words that make up the sentence "Don't judge a book by it's cover" I found a strange formula coagulated before my eyes. It came out like this:

"Test a text book pass by over view while judging grounds coverage."

And when you are reading the Bible you have to ask yourself "What am I reading this for, do I want to know about the history of Creation or do I want t o know what God believes in?" So I skipped from the first page straight to where I thought I could find what God believes in. The Ten Commandments and I test a text book pass by overview while judging ground coverage and I get this:

Thou shall not...

Thou shall not...

Thou shall not...

Two words should stand out to you and those words are "Kill and Steal" but most of all Steal.

I meditated on this word because it caused me great worry as to why God would introduce it to my vocabulary when the world was so much simpler without it. I also wondered how anything My God doesn't believe in even exist?

Knock and the door shall be opened.

When I spent a few seconds contemplating any hidden teachings that the word steal might hold I witnessed a great miracle explaining the parable of "If you give a man a fish" and I know this also to be true…

God could have said "Thou shall have values and not give them away" but that would be giving them away.

Instead, He made us ponder His wonders and excavate, earning the worthiness of His value which would have been cheapened had He just given it to us.

When you have to seek for value you are adding to the enrichment of that value therefore making it more valuable.

He also explained to me why the pen is mightier than the sword. The sword is just a sharpened chunk of metal whose materials can be refined anywhere in the Earth's crust, but if it wasn't for the line that ties the bond from the page through the pen to the writer's hand the pen would be extinguished from ever being in existence. Hence the word "steal" is proof that God exists because He made it up just to teach us that lesson..

Peace is also a bad word because if it didn't exist neither would it's opposite.

Chapter 10

One Man's Trash Is Another Man's Floating Junk

I found a couple more invisible scroll lessons by utilizing this random access thumb through the Bible method. On one occasion I flipped to a page and the first thing that caught my eyes read:

Thou shall not worship Witches, Warlocks or Wizards. If you happen to spend some time on the puzzle "Read between the lines" and discover the SkyLight Blue Book you will have the ability to look up artifacts like The Leather Bound Button Snap Lock Pick Pocket Book as well as many other objects that might be of use on your quest.

The skylight blue book is an astral plane book with light blue pages. Just imagine a hotel ledger or a captain's log with columns for name, picture and description and you should be able to find whatever it is that comes to mind that you're looking for.

I hate to plagiarize but some entries from that Catalog are just too juicy for me to leave out.

I'm referring to the entries I found involving lycanthropes and werewolves:

"Werewolves are all generic mere life forms that tap pastries for their hints of trace elements that are their life's force." "They are first crusade dedicates on a quest for the cures and salves for their curse of unquenchable thirst for God's knowledge."

Tap pastries, All generic mere (alergic to mirrors), hints and trace not to mention first aid kit those entries really tickled my fancy.

The answer to that "What water fowl that left its tracks behind in the first letter of the Bible" riddle was crane, you get it? The capital letter "I" sounds like Caterpillar which is a kind of construction crane. And cranes leave <u>tracks</u> at construction sites. But I bet you already knew that.

Do you see how werewolves are related to that riddle? Because they are allergic to meres and tapestries and tracing elements like paper all leading up to the construction crane from the riddle. Construction paper.

If you are unable to see the skylight blue book catalog for whatever reason, maybe you don't have the confidence or you might have a fear of seeing invisible things, try looking up "Talisman" and you might be surprised at the wheel of fortune puzzle there is to solve.

Another time I flipped to a random page and the only words I needed from that experiment were the two "Silver Chairs." I got a vision of collapsible business recliners and The Rocking Carousel Horse that to me symbolized a great war being played out between corporate businesses and the lower and middle classes average Joe.

Money is a necessary Evil that has advanced mankind as far as it can technologically, socially and medically but it is an outdated concept Good should have the power to overcome.

I'm just going to rapid fire off a couple of invisible scrolls I'm not sure of where they came from. Floating Junk.

"A period decal spells ends of sentence dialog supplying a parallel parameter between the start of a hard sentence and the end of a rough course."

"In order for a word to be awarded as a reward in service it must pass down sentence dialog in cross references to direction and distances between obstacles and objectives."

"Judge a scrolls context by plain English proper letter form and sentence structure."

There are a lot of old fashion plane references in that last one starting with the word "context." For those that don't know "Contact!" is the word we used to yell when we had to start our push motor planes back in the day.

Here is the most profound invisible scroll I ever witnessed and I think it shows the lengths that God would go through just to tell a good one. I was just phasing out one day and saw these words scroll across a wall I was staring at. If you ask me this scroll is about the difference between myself and Jesus!

"Why would ever endeavor up a hill,

Go following along fellow Jack, Lady Jill

To quench their thirst for a drink of well water,

When every village Lassie or Lad adorned with a golden eye for water retrieval knows…

Never did dew drops of rain water fall up?"

If you know a little more about how Jack broke his crown you might find an amulet in these words that follow the last line.

"Express news prints Jack kicks a hand stand."

I'm certain that the vision of how the world began was the truth and that these invisible scrolls are what God armed me with to back up that claim.

The Mystery of the
2 Champions'
Wine Glasses

The last thing I remember seeing before the vision ended was a mystery to solve called the mystery of the 2 champions' wine glasses.

The only hint to it is a picture of two hands holding up their glasses in a toast. If you look closely it's easy to see that the outline of the fingers holding up the glasses resemble a man and a woman facing each other. If you look even closer you'll see also that the splash of wine in the air above the glasses resembles a man and a woman's bodies intertwined. This is the image God created man after.

I think I have already solved this mystery and it has something to do with one of the orders I am passing down from my father. The one about working every other day shifts.

By putting everybody on an every other day schedule you wake up everyday in a different world.

Some people would work Monday, Wednesday and Friday while others would have Tuesday, Thursday and Saturday with everybody off on the Sabbath. So once a week you still get 2 days off in a row either Saturday and Sunday or Sunday and Monday.

The days you get to go to work is your chance to contribute your light to the world but what is one light in a sea of lights.

The days you have off you have the chance to shine that light on your immediate family, close friends and relative acquaintances like God's heat lamp incubating your clutch.

One of these days you might wake up in a world where nothing else existed but the person who means the world to you. Maybe that day would land on a Sunday when everybody gets the day off.

The Mystery of the Silverchairs

One day I decided to just flip to any page in the Bible and look, scan the page until I got a bead on something and when I did I found this "Silverchairs."

Not much at first but upon further meditation I found prolific results including the rocking carousel horse and the collapsable business recliners.

Anyways, one model involved the world ending with over kill of businesses up in penthouse suites of high rise buildings complete with dust covered business furniture and the other model, the motto for our hero, the rocking carousel horse, goes:

> I am the point all
> rays of light
> must come pass
> and
> All land turns on

The B.A.D.D.
(Blue Angels/Dare Devils)
Will Lift
The F.O.G
(Family of God)

Would you believe that Red and Blue represent the Brotherhood and Sisterhood in the Family of God?

Always has and always will.

But the devil tried to trick us into using our own colors against ourselves when he created the Bloods and Crips.

I'm sick of all of these religious cults where they bring you in and tell you to look up to someone else. Shouldn't they be teaching you to look up to yourself?

I think what God wants is us to worship each other. Why else would He have gone through so much trouble to create a world with so many pitfalls of true love?

The concept of matrimony and the institution of marriage seems to be the biggest pitfalls of them all. From a very young age we are not taught but coaxed into the idea that there is a perfect match for us somewhere waiting to be found and one day we'll find each other, fall into love's everlasting stronghold of intimacy and live happily ever after.

But that makes it easy for one to imagine the perfect match and what ends up happening is we take the first person we meet and give them the persauna of our perfect match and at the very least our hearts and souls are damaged when the truth about who they really are comes into the light.

If life is really about the journey and the soulmates we meet along the way then I think we shouldn't fool ourselves into believing our true love will even be born in the same country we are born in.

We shouldn't have high hopes about how good looking, kind and sweet our other halves may be. I think the concept of marriage evokes those thoughts giving us expectations of how our counterparts should act or even look. How can you have predetermined standards of someone you haven't even met yet?

Anyways, with the Family of God separated into the 2 sects, Blue Angels and Dare Devils, we would have each other to thank for looking out for one another and helping us find our way to the Kingdom of True Love.

Not that any one of us is perfect but that it takes a village to make the right mistakes!

Can you imagine a world where everybody was in either sect of the church, striving to someday achieve the title of Blue Angel or Dare Devil?

I imagine a world where there are 2 squads on deck based on how we interact with each other in 3 man teams called Darts. Each unit would have someone to be either the Flight, Shaft or Tip and depending on what each agent's specialty was would be assigned to go on specific missions.

That last paragraph was TMI. Don't throw out the rest of the book based on my observations made in this chapter. I know what to do, I'll tell you the most messed up story of Jesus Christ I can think of!

I don't know how this story came to be in my subconscious. All I know is that it could be the worst thing ever published about Jesus. Bad publicity is still publicity so here it goes.

The world was still in its caveman stage and there was no such thing as religion yet, there was only total chaos. But even in total chaos the odds of someone having a vision close to the true Kingdom of Heaven are astronomical to one. Let's say 8,976,251,545,100:1. That's astronomical enough. Throw in a few more zero's and you get my point. But there is still a chance. And that 1 in a billion shot came in the form of John the Baptist.

He was famous for traveling the countryside and converting nonbelievers. I guess the first couple of people were easy to convert but eventually John needed the mark to trust John with his life and John found that submerging his victim under water was a sufficient way to get the message across. You can think of him as the One Man Army of God.

The crowds that John would draw started getting bigger and bigger, an easy target for pickpockets in The Den of Thieves to prey upon.

The only problem was John never stayed in one place for too long and all kinds of resources were exhausted by The Den of Thieves on keeping up with John's traveling up and down the country.

One day a member of the Den of Thieves had an epiphany! We should make up our own shows and draw the crowds to us. Everybody agreed it was the best plan of action and went along with the plan.

But how do you think God would act if someone was to take advantage of His only soldier's reputation. The only feet God has on the ground in this war was John the Baptist and now this would give him a bad name.

But instead of punish the person for this underhanded act, God took mercy upon him and gave him the power to perform miracles making him His own son.

Thank Jesus because without him the world would be still fighting with sticks and stones over borders and the game would never be winnable. I would probably have spent my whole life to convince the country I was born in that I'm the pass ages message sender then died with the rest of the world unreached.

Come on. Doesn't that make you want to become a Blue Angel or Dare Devil like 30 times more than you did before you read it? I am going to stir up some trouble, all I want to know is "Who's coming with me?" It's better than the green team vs. the red team with the dinosaurs.

Shouts out to my first two victims, just kidding, I mean members to the B.A.D.D. FAMILY OF GOD Gigi Santos formerly known as Benita Thomas and Mr. December a.k.a Reginald Raines. Thank you for believing in me and for being good, going hard and being on my team. I know if the world ends now I'll have you both on my side no matter what else goes wrong. God bless.

Announcing…

His Eminence's Anonymous
Foundation

To bring Heaven on Earth

Goals: To support sciences and concepts like those found in this
book. Get this ship running like clock work on every other day
schedules. Never work 2 days in a row for the rest of eternity!

Proceeds to be spent on "once every ten year parties"
where the world gets to make up 10 new laws that
and festivities for said event ceremony.

Find us on Gofundme
for donation information please contact me
anthonyrobertlasham@gmail.com

Receive a Rocking Carousel Horse Protection Against
Evil Charm for every donation of $50 or more.

www.ingramcontent.com/pod-product-compliance
Lightning Source LLC
Chambersburg PA
CBHW021914040426
42447CB00007B/845